# PRAISE FOR 'WHEN GOD SAYS NO'

These raw and naked writings reveal the unquenchable, patient love between a mother and her precious son. Within every page is fresh hope for the most difficult situation, and a gentle wind of grace to lift up the weary and carry one straight into the arms of the One who heals the broken and the hurting.

*Nancy J. Grandquist*
*Author and Speaker*

———⚬⚬⚬———

We know one of the secrets of Denise Wynn's spiritual life...

She has called on Jesus more in one day than some do in one month!

Journey with Denise and her family as they are transformed by anguish, aloneness, and angel visitations.

*David S. Norris, Ph.D, Professor (Urshan Graduate School of Theology); and Nancy Norris, Ed.D, Adjunct Faculty (Urshan Graduate School of Theology)*

No...Such a small word, but so definitive. A road block on the way to what we wanted. No way around, "No."

It stops you in your tracks.

In disappointed determination, we look for every possible way to get around this road block, but our efforts are futile. It is then that we discover the only way to see clearly is up! When God says, "no," grace will flow! For whatever He withholds, He makes up for it by giving strength, understanding, and relationship. So if life lands you in a dark hole that seems like a tomb for all your dreams, look up. There is LIFE beyond the tragedy. Denise has lived it, and lived it well. She can teach you what to do if you have been trusted with a tragedy. Her beautiful smile is proof.

*Thetus Tenney*
*Author and Speaker, Focused Light Ministries*

Denise Wynn reveals her innermost struggles in this heart-rending narrative of raising a child diagnosed with Autism. The Center for Disease Control currently reports that one in 88 children are diagnosed with this devastating disorder that affects families, schools, and communities. Every 11 minutes, another child is diagnosed with Autism.

One of the most striking, yet true statements that Denise makes is this: "Many Christians have great difficulty accepting the fact that chronic illnesses exist within the church."

With a pained heart, I have watched as "normal" children shunned children with Autism and I have also observed adults showed impatience through their actions. If one child out of 88 children is diagnosed with Autism, it is highly possible that there are families suffering with this illness in your congregation. I pray that this book will help us to understand the agony these families are going through and that we will find ways to be supportive rather than judgmental.

Thank you, Denise, for climbing your mountain one step at a time, for sharing your journey with us, and for the strong faith you exhibited through that journey. You have raised an awareness with this book that has touched my heart and I know it will touch the hearts of all who read it.

*Gwyn Oakes*
*Ladies Ministries President*
*United Pentecostal Church International*

———∞∞∞———

At last, an autism book that tells the story of the suffering that families endure and the courage they show when their children are in crisis and in desperate need of services. The author's firsthand account of the process and pain of placing a child in a residential program is graphic, engrossing and enlightening. A must read for families in need and those who care about them.

*Lisa McCauley Parles, Esquire*

# *When God Says No*

## FINDING THE FAITH TO ACCEPT GOD'S WILL
### DENISE WYNN

---

*For Sean, my beautiful boy:*
*you have taught me what truly matters,*
*changed the way I think about everything,*
*and caused me to live daily in the presence of God.*

---

# CONTENTS

# Contents

# ACKNOWLEDGEMENTS

They say it takes a village to raise a child. I say it takes a special village to raise a child with special needs. I am fortunate to know many super incredible human beings with extraordinary qualities. Superheroes do exist.

*To Sean's Special Education Superheroes from GCSSS, ACSSS and Bancroft:* you fill his days with challenges and rewards, and are always striving to help him do his best. *To the Bancroft residential staff:* I thank you for caring for my son with integrity, kindness and compassion.

*To the many family, friends, and acquaintances over the years who have significantly blessed my boy's life (and even strangers who worked in school or met Sean in the community):* I want to say, "Thank you" from my heart.

*To the More to Life Mom's group:* many years have passed since we began our journey into the "New World." You are my heart sisters forever.

*Acknowledgements*

*To Nancy Eshelman, our neighbor and friend:* you are a treasure. Thank you for everything you have given to our family.

*To my work friends:* you have seen me cry and then made me laugh, because we all know, "No one cares." Yoli, I know that God planned the exact moment we would meet.

*To Rachel Neyland:* you were the best babysitter ever! To the Killingsworth family: you have seen it all and love us anyway. I cherish our friendship.

*To Ron, Roseanne, Rachelle and Ronnie Spatafore:* our family has been blessed by your faithful and so-much-fun friendship.

*To Cindy Miller:* you are my best and forever friend, therapist, cheer leader, and the one who saw more in me than I ever believed existed. LuLu, you are always right.

*To my parents, Edward and Jane Gay:* there are not enough words... You have always been there. The way you love each of your children and grandchildren is truly selfless, generous and unconditional. *To my siblings, Eddie, Heather, and Kim:* I know you love me and you know I love you...somehow this alone works for us. *To Wayne and Josie, my in-love-laws:* thank you for all of your hands-on help and loving support.

*To Aaron:* you are more than I could have dreamed possible in a son. I am grateful for every, "YES" that God has granted us in you. *To Gary:* I am so glad that we did not become one of the 85% of couples whose marriages disintegrate under the stress of raising a child with disabilities. Through it all, we are stronger, better, and more in love than ever. You are an incredible dad, a faithful husband, and a beautiful man.

*To Steven D'Amico Jr.:* thank you for doing what might have killed me.

*When God Says No*

*To the Cornetts, the Raymonds and my Spirit and Truth family:* It's a privilege to share this journey with you. Never in a million years did I imagine that Gary and I would be working alongside you. Thank you for loving us.

I could not have written this book without a wonderful, talented, hyper-skilled editor. Krystal Mayville, I am certain that no one on the planet could have kept my voice as authentic as you have. You have the gift of "Krystalization." Powerful! You "succinct" me AND you are so much fun to work with. Without you, I would not have found Cara Davis, graphic designer extraordinaire! Cara, you "got me" from the onset and made it all real.

This book has been inside of me for many years, waiting for a happy ending before being shared with you. Thank you, God, for showing me that some stories are meant to be told just as they are. The miracle is found in the knowledge that YOU are the beginning and the end of every story. My Alpha and My Omega, I love you.

# INTRODUCTION

*"But others were tortured, refusing to turn from God in order to be set free. They placed their hope in a better life after the resurrection. Some were jeered at, and their backs were cut open with whips. Others were chained in prisons. Some died by stoning, some were sawed in half, and others were killed with the sword. Some went about wearing skins of sheep and goats, destitute and oppressed and mistreated. They were too good for this world, wandering over deserts and mountains, hiding in caves and holes in the ground. All these people earned a good reputation because of their faith, yet none of them received all that God had promised. For God had something better in mind for us, so that they would not reach perfection without us." Hebrews 11:35-39*

It is not often preached. As a matter of fact, in twenty-three years of Sunday sermons, Bible studies, care groups, camp meetings and conferences, I have only ever heard the end of Hebrews read aloud one time. My pastor, Stan Miller, a man who knows what a NO from

God feels like, preached a message from those scriptures and from his life that healed a very broken piece of my heart.

God always answers prayer. His answers arrive in a variety of ways. My personal favorite (and I'm guessing yours too) is the immediate, "Yes, Sweet One! Here you go. You are welcome! Enjoy!"

Then there's the, "Okay, but you have to wait," answer. We don't love this one, but it is doable because we know that what we desire will eventually come to us.

Next is the, "No," which we often misconceive as, "Okay, but wait." Finally, if we do not receive the answer we pleaded for, we sometimes interpret that as no answer at all.

Sometimes, however, No just means No. The Lord God Almighty, The Great Big Wonderful, Omnipotent One in His Majestic, Omniscient Sovereignty, says, "NO."

When we feel like God is not answering our prayers, frustration builds as our faith repeatedly rises and falls. Waiting for a yes from heaven takes our hearts to new places as we imagine and dream the best and worst of scenarios.

Unanswered prayers can lead to disappointment in God, causing us to conjure up great feats of manipulation, self-loathing, poor coping skills and self-inflicted wounds.

Hearing and understanding the word, "No," has allowed me to move forward to a place where I have found God to be very different than the one I thought I knew. He keeps his promises and His grace is enough. He is always present, even when I am weeping into my pillow, screaming into the heavens, or completely ignoring Him. He watches over His precious, pitiful daughter with unfailing love, mercy, and compassion.

In my surrender to His will, I have seen glimpses of His power and purpose. Accepting the NO has allowed doors of ministry to open where I have since been blessed to touch the wounded, comfort the afflicted, and encourage the brokenhearted.

Most importantly, accepting the NO has shown me how much I long for Heaven. Sean's disabilities remind me that I live in a fallen world which is not my home.

———&&&———

*"...All these people earned a good reputation because of their faith, yet none of them received all that God had promised...For God had some-thing better in mind for us." Hebrews 11:39-40*

———&&&———

There is a fine line between faith and acceptance. This is the tight-rope that we, who live at the end of Hebrews, Chapter 11, must walk.

# FOREWORD

Dear Reader,

You are holding a book that has the potential to open your eyes, heal your heart, restore your faith in God, or possibly do all three… depending on your need. This is a special book. You were drawn to it for a reason.

I first met Denise when our ministries became intertwined years ago. She was a young mother, full of passion for God, with a vision for ministry. I was the president of our denomination's New Jersey/Delaware District Women's Division, and had invited this talented visionary to serve on my committee. After a period of time, Denise and Gary relocated to work with us in our growing church. This family included their elder son, Aaron, and younger son, Sean. Sean, with his special needs, captured the hearts of our church family. Sean's Friends was formed and members of this team provided complete care for Sean at church. During these years of ministry partnership, we began to see firsthand the demanding 24/7 responsibility and care that this precious family had with their darling boy.

Over the years, I have been privileged to be a close friend of Denise and to share the ups and downs of her journey, upon which the writings in this book are based. My friend is painfully honest, laugh out loud funny, and deeply reflective. For those who love and care for people who require more than most will ever give in a relationship, this book will resonate with you. For those who have family or friends with special needs, please read this book in order to understand how to be a better friend and a more supportive family member. And for those who sit in churches and look across the congregation at families who have a child, brother, sister, mother, father, or anyone else with special needs, please read this to gain perspective on how to minister to them.

*When God Says No* is a work of bold courage and raw honesty. Denise's anecdotal style is captivating and inviting. Read her story with an open heart and prepare to be changed.

Now turn the page and begin your journey.

*Cindy Miller, Ph.D. (abd)*
*Author, Counselor, Pastor and Professor*

# A NOTE TO THE READER

The stories I have written in this book are such a small part of the eighteen years that I have been Sean's mom. I have attempted to bring you into my life at the lowest and worst to show you my heart with raw authenticity. There may be times that I appear cynical, sarcastic, disrespectful and even mean. While I admit to feeling these characteristics, I have never allowed them to embed into my soul.

I have learned the beauty of forgiveness, acceptance and grace, and I am certain that it is only by the great and amazing grace of God that I still stand. The Lord only knows which ward in the psychiatric hospital would be my home, were it not for His faithfulness to me.

He has rescued me from the edge when I was sure I would fall, crashing to a million pieces. I have spent hours in the darkness, sitting and rocking on the floor, fighting for my sanity, wailing and moaning when too grieved to pray. I have felt the spirit of fear paralyze me. I met the spirit of suicide while crossing over a bridge. I have carried the dark cloud of depression and experienced the suffocating breathlessness of anxiety. I have faced death on every level, the death of body, soul and spirit, but each time I rose again with the resolve to live another day.

With every victory, I have become stronger and more determined to live a life that matters. I want my life to count for something so much greater than mere existence. It has to be a life that ministers this solid truth to others: that God is able to do exceedingly abundantly above all that we are able to ask or think, according to the power that works in us.

Heart to heart, from me to you, I pray that you are encouraged and inspired.

*Denise Wynn*

*"For this light momentary affliction is preparing for us an eternal weight of glory beyond all comparison."*
*II Corinthians 4:17*

# CHAPTER ONE

## *THE SOUND OF SIRENS*

# THE SOUND OF SIRENS

I had always imagined that my grown up life would be happy. Boy meets girl, they fall in love, get married, buy the house with the picket fence and have babies. I was a believer in all things good. Why not? My life had always been good. I enjoyed an average childhood in a 1970's suburbia with a loving family. I married the man of my dreams and together we fell in love with Jesus. Vowing to love one another and deeply committed to our faith, surely our "happily ever after" was guaranteed.

My first pregnancy gave us a beautiful, healthy baby boy who has been a joy from the moment he was born. Aaron was sweet, adorable, loving and good-natured. He was such a blessing and we wanted another. Of course we completely expected that we would get what we wanted.

Three years later, we had our second son, Sean, another beautiful, healthy bundle of joy. Everything was great until the morning I heard the strangest, scariest sound I had ever heard. I ran to his room and found my baby shaking and seizing in his crib. I picked him up, ran to the phone and called 9-1-1.

The paramedics arrived. My baby was lying there, unresponsive, and his skin had turned a pale shade of bluish grey. They hurriedly strapped an oxygen mask to his face, placed him onto the gurney and ushered me into the back of the ambulance. With sirens blaring and lights flashing, we arrived at the nearest hospital.

This scenario of sirens, ambulance rides, paramedics, doctors, nurses and hospitals became our new life. We had entered a brand new world, so different than anything we had ever known. It was scary and chaotic. The people were different, the language was different, and everything that I saw and felt in the atmosphere was foreign to me.

On two previous occasions before that grand mal seizure came and changed our lives forever, I had suspected that something was wrong with Sean. There was the time he was limp and lethargic and we took him to the emergency room. The doctor told us that he had an ear infection. Then there was the morning I attended a ladies' prayer meeting and Sean's arm appeared to be twitching. An experienced mother of five assured me that he was just trying to roll over. In each instance, without any reason at all, my internal voice of instinct whispered, "seizure." Then, within 24 hours of his six month wellness doctor visit, Sean had his first full blown grand mal seizure.

Sean's seizures began to occur weekly. Medication was started and visits with the neurology department at Children's Hospital of Phila-delphia (CHOP) were scheduled. The team at CHOP was fantastic. Sean had a series of EEG's, PET scans, MRI and CAT scans, and chromosomal testing. There were no traces of physiological evidence for his seizure disorder, which gave us much hope that his convulsions were febrile in nature, and he would outgrow them. Since both my father and I had febrile seizures as children, I simply suspected that Sean's convulsions were also febrile seizures. However, this was not to be true for us. Sean was diagnosed with epilepsy.

# CHAPTER TWO

## *FROM BAD TO WORSE*

# FROM BAD TO WORSE

S tatus Epilepticus (SE) is a life-threatening condition in which the brain is in a state of persistent seizure. This monster seizure shows up sometimes as one continuous, unremitting seizure, lasting longer than five minutes. Other times, the seizures are recurrent, leaving a person unconscious between seizures for several minutes. Treatment usually starts after the seizure has lasted five minutes. It is considered a medical emergency. Seizures are not likely to stop in that five minute span without medical intervention and five minutes is sufficient time for neurological damage to occur. If the status seizure is not stabilized quickly, the risk of death is increased.

Sean was nine months old when he had his first life-threatening episode of Status Epilepticus. We were at my parent's house celebrating my sister's birthday. I was sitting in the living room with Sean when the seizure began. It ended after a few minutes and then another one started. I had not seen this happen before. Someone called 9-1-1 and the ambulance arrived quickly. Sean was still seizing as the paramedics placed him onto the gurney and into the back of the rig. I climbed into the ambulance as instructed, and answered their questions as we sped toward the hospital.

I heard the EMT call the Emergency Room to inform them of the situation. When we arrived, a medical crew waited outside and immediately rushed Sean in through the doors. I was stopped and again asked to answer the same questions I had already answered. I watched from a distance as nursing staff surrounded my baby, frantically opening drawers and cabinets and running down the hall grabbing plastic bags with tubes and syringes. I heard the words, "Code Blue ER," repeated several times over the intercom, but did not realize that we were the code blue, until a small army of medical staff came running down the hallway into my child's room.

The next thing I remember was my husband standing at my side while a doctor told us that they had made arrangements to have Sean transported to Cooper Trauma Center by the MediVac Helicopter. Everything happened so fast. Sean's little body was still seizing. It had been nearly forty minutes since the onset of this seizure. He was placed into the ambulance once again and taken to the helicopter waiting in a nearby location. We were told to meet them at the trauma center.

Some moments are forever burned into your memory. This ride is one of them. Searing pain accompanied the thought of losing someone I loved more than my own life. Panic, grief, hope, fear, and hope again cycled through our minds as we drove 45 minutes to the city of Camden. One prayer chanted repeatedly, "Please let him live, please let him live, please let him live...."

Upon our arrival, we were escorted to the trauma unit where we waited for the news. Not knowing if our baby was dead or alive, every second felt like a long journey where I was repeatedly climbing up a steep, rocky hill and then falling back down. Finally, someone said the words we desperately needed to hear:"Your son is stabilized... critical but stable." Then I saw him as he was wheeled into the unit in a large metal crib. He was attached to a ventilator that pushed air into his lungs through a tube to keep him alive. His curly, baby-fine blonde hair had been shaved and there was an intravenous needle in the side of his head. He was unconscious, but he was alive!

As soon as Sean regained consciousness, he shook the ventilator tube loose and pulled the IV from his head. We were amazed at his strength and resilience. He recovered quickly and was ready to go home just days later. Our baby was such a fighter.

I was so relieved to have my sweet boy in my arms again. I never considered or even thought to ask if any brain damage may have occurred during the hour-long seizure. Much later, I would research the fact that deprivation of oxygen to the brain during prolonged seizure activity may cause damage to neurons, cognitive impairment, developmental delay and an increased occurrence of autism in children who are diagnosed with a seizure disorder.

There was so much that I didn't know. I was innocent, naive, young, and so hopeful that God would hear my prayers. I was completely unaware of the multitude of battles that would come, or that my baby would have to fight to live through Status Epilepticus eleven more times.

## CHAPTER THREE

*THE FIRST TIME GOD SAID NO*

*Disappointment. It comes in waves. An ebb and flow of emotions seemingly so strategic as to allow one to touch the brink of insanity or despair, but not quite cross over the delicate edge.*

———— ✺ ————

# THE FIRST TIME GOD SAID NO

I remember the first time God said No. We were told that an evangelist, well-known for practicing in the gifts of healing, was scheduled to be at a church in our area. We knew we needed a miracle and we believed that God was the Healer. My husband, Gary, and I packed up our son, Sean, and took him to the service. We sang praise and worship songs in our car, praying all the way there. Our faith was building, and with each mile we drove, we were closer to our miracle. During the worship service and again during the preaching, we felt such anticipation. The preacher told story after story of miracles and healings. He pointed to people in the congregation and discerned their sicknesses and told them they were healed. When they took up an offering, we were told to give according to our faith so that we would receive our miracle. We only had $300 in the bank, but we knew God would honor our sacrifice if we gave all we had, because that's what the preacher had said. Eagerly, we placed our check in the offering plate and then stepped out of the pew, into the aisle where the healing line had already formed.

We waited and watched as one-by-one, the minister laid his hands on people's heads, praying earnestly and specifically for their needs, often knowing their ailment without being told. I knew for sure he would call out the epileptic spirit when he prayed for my son. As we got closer to the preacher, Gary and I began thanking God for our son's healing. The preacher quickly touched Sean's head and said, "Be healed in Jesus' name," and then he moved past us to the next person in line. Disappointment swelled inside of me as we walked away from the healing line. I looked up at one of the stained glass windows in the church and saw a picture of Jesus holding a chubby blonde baby boy (with an incredible resemblance to my son) in his arms. Inside my head, I heard Him say, "I have not healed Sean, but I am holding Him."

God said No. We got ripped off. I wanted our money back.

Sean's seizures got worse, life went on, and the prayer lines continued. On many occasions, I was called out in front of everyone during church services, to come to the front and pray. I was pulled out of my pew and accosted with oil and prayer. I was also advised to sleep with prayer cloths on all my pillows and to pin prayer cloths to my baby's clothes, all of which I did with obedience and a lingering sense of hope. Prayer lines, healing evangelists, and miracle crusades remain touchy subjects for me to this day.

Through the years I have watched, commiserated with, and pitied my fellow chronically-afflicted brothers and sisters. None so much, however, as one saint who was involved in a horrible car accident which crushed both of her ankles. Every service, I watched her lean on her walker and faithfully hobble up to sit on the front row, waiting for her miracle. She had held out a long time, waiting on the front row for God to miraculously re-create her bones (as she was told He would do by many well-meaning people). She finally agreed to allow the doctors to fuse her ankles and implant steel rods. Week after week, those same well-meaning people would try to pull her up out of her chair, encouraging her to step out in faith. As time went by, there sat the poor Sister. The pastor began to get frustrated with her lack of faith, and would command that she walk and even demand that she run. She tried to please him. Once she was physically able, she would stand with her walker and shuffle back and forth in the altar area. It was excruciating to watch. I wanted her to shuffle right out the front door and find a church that would simply accept her disability and love her without condition.

Many Christians have great difficulty accepting the fact that chronic illnesses exist within the church.

One of my best friends has Type I Diabetes, as does her daughter. I have stood with her in the healing lines as she waited for the evangelist to touch her with the anointing oil so that she would be healed. On one occasion, she was so confident that God had healed her that she refused to use her insulin. Months later, when faced with the decision to either resume her insulin or go into a diabetic coma (which would ultimately result in death), she chose the medication. Some would say it was a lack of faith, but I have seen what great faith it takes to live with a chronic illness. I have watched my friend and her daughter count the carbohydrates in every single morsel of food they put in their mouths. All day, every day, they have dealt with needles, ports and pumps. Trust me when I say nobody wanted them to be healed more than they did.

I have attended funerals of faithful Christians who believed until they took their last breath, that God would heal them. Others have died suddenly without a prayer. I have stood beside the caskets of the elderly, who had lived good, long lives, smiling as we retold stories and recounted memories. I have cried beside the caskets of middle aged friends, who still had so much more living to do. I have wept beside the caskets of teenagers, who had only just begun to enjoy life. I have grieved beside the caskets of children surrounded by stuffed animals, who barely knew life. Some suffered long and painful deaths while others were gone in an instant, without warning.

Sometimes God just says No.

# CHAPTER FOUR

## *YOU DON'T TRUST ME*

# YOU DON'T TRUST ME

Praying was as easy as breathing. I was so desperate for strength to get through my days that I prayed constantly, and always my prayers circled back to Sean. On and on, over and over, I prayed the same prayer, sometimes begging, and often demanding. I always instructed God to do it my way. Honestly, I thought my plan was brilliant. I knew that God could do it, and I believed that He would. After twelve episodes of Status Epilepticus in just one year's time, it was miraculous that Sean was even alive! Surely, God, a complete healing would bring you the glory you deserve. All eyes are on You, The Great Big, Wonderful, Amazing, Awesome, All-Powerful Creator of the Universe! Come on, God. You can do this!

As I was loudly cheering God on in prayer, He quietly whispered, "You don't trust me."

At this point, I really believed that God would heal my child. I thought that I completely trusted Him, but this particular conversation with the Lord changed everything I believed about what it means to trust. As I continued my attempt to persuade the Almighty that I trusted Him, He illuminated my mind with a concept so strange to me, that I physically recoiled from the shock. He said, "You trust that I will heal your child, but you do not trust me if I don't." I took a moment to consider this statement, asking myself if

19

I could accept His will. I visualized my baby in the ICU, and then in a casket, and I decided that I could not trust God because I did not know what He would do. The conversation ended, a wall was erected, and although I went through the motions of prayer, God and I stopped talking that day.

Life went on, and at times I would give in to my desperation and ask God for help. My prayers became requests, always one-sided. I was careful not to linger in His presence for fear that He would say something...or anything at all. It is difficult to be a non-praying Christian, but I became excellent at it. Praying for others still worked. People still received the Holy Spirit with my untrusting hand on their shoulder. I was faithful and attended every scheduled prayer meeting. I just made sure that I did all of the talking during each prayer. I did not want to hear what God had to say.

Sean's seizures worsened. They became more frequent and sometimes occurred multiple times a day. We tried several different treatments and he was hospitalized often as we made changes to his medications. Eventually his neurologist found a combination of anti-convulsants that limited his seizure activity to one time per week and stopped the life-threatening Status episodes. Sweet relief! This was not the healing I had desired, but it was manageable.

As my fears began to subside, my longing for the Lord increased. I felt the empty place immediately when I was able to start feeling again. The effort of holding up the wall between us became too much for me. One Sunday afternoon, I went to the front of the church to pray. I walked to the pastor, intending to reveal my heart, ask for prayer, and finally close the distance between me and God. As I stood before him with tears running down my face, attempting to describe my need, he stopped me and said, "You know what your problem is? Your prayer life stinks!" Then he repeated it louder so that others within earshot wouldn't miss his discernment of my sin. "YOUR PRAYER LIFE STINKS!"

The force of his words, both literally and spiritually, stunned me. I was so hurt, embarrassed, and even less trusting of God for having told on me and for allowing this man to hurt me, shame me, and expose me with what I thought was my secret.

Honestly, it was a very long time before I was able to pray again. I became a fake Christian. I looked it and I lived it, but my heart was sealed shut. God was right. I did not trust Him.

## CHAPTER FIVE

## *THE DAY THE WORDS WENT AWAY*

# THE DAY THE WORDS WENT AWAY

S ean was two years and four months old when his words left. He
had just started saying, "I love you."

I remember my panic growing, hour by hour, as Seany moved about
silently that entire day. No words! There was no, "Mommy, Daddy, or
Aaara," (for Aaron). There were also no meal time prayers of, "Jesus,
Jesus, Amen!" that he usually spoke so enthusiastically after happily
devouring each bite.

I called his neurologist at the Children's Hospital. He asked to see
Sean immediately. He believed that the loss of language was po-
tentially related to Sean's anti-convulsant medication, Phenobarbi-
tal. We took Sean in for an exam, and then started him on a new
medication, with high hopes that his words would quickly return.
Still, no words came. Instead, he started having more seizures. We
watched as two, and sometimes three seizures per day, shook his little body. At that point, due to the traumatic nature of the seizures,
we stopped focusing on the fact that his words had not returned,
until the day came when we were introduced to an uncomfortable,
new word called Autism.

We had attended a family gathering, where we spent some time with
my brother-in-law, Brian, and his wife, Melissa. Later, they men-

tioned to my mother-in-law that they were concerned something might be wrong with Sean. As they compared Sean to Melissa's young nephew, they realized that Sean was significantly developmentally delayed.

My instincts blared. Loud, hot waves of panic seethed through my mind. I quickly wrapped my panic in offense so that I could absorb the information and process it logically. It is easy to be offended, but to look at the possibility that your child is somehow defective, damaged, and "not normal" is not easy. But I knew that they were right. Something was very wrong.

As one silent day followed another and odd behaviors continued to emerge, I made an appointment with a developmental psychologist at the Seashore House in Philadelphia. As we waited for the doctor, Sean sat quietly on the floor, lining up his toy cars and crackers in two perfectly straight rows, repeatedly making careful and constant adjustments to the straightness of each line. It was in that dimly lit, stuffy, small exam room that a doctor with the ugliest, bushiest eyebrows that I had ever seen, looked into my eyes and impaled my heart with one word: "Autism."

"Your child has Autism," he told us. Shock, horror, disbelief, and grief enveloped us as we thought, "No. There is no way this is true."

"Does he walk on his toes?"

"Yes."

"Does he flap his hands?"

"Yes, sometimes."

"Does he often line up objects in a straight row?"

"Yes."

"Does he talk?"

"No."

"Does he play with other children?"

"No."

"Does he ever reach for you?"

"No."

Autism had abducted my little boy, just two years and four months into his little life. The seizures continued, and just as the psychologist had predicted, Sean's developmental delays emerged.

What a difference one day makes. All of his words left. They had completely vanished. Suddenly in their place was a plethora of odd-looking hand-flapping, finger-twirling, and head-banging, accompanied by the ever-present tiptoed walking.

Grabbing, pinching, scratching, and ear-piercing shrieking soon followed and settled in for good, and became Sean's only means of communication.

# CHAPTER SIX

## *FATHER ABRAHAM*

*"Some time later, God tested Abraham's faith. "Abraham!"
God called. "Yes," he replied. "Here I am." "Take your son,
your only son - yes, Isaac, whom you love so much - and
go to the land of Moriah. Go and sacrifice him as a burnt
offering on one of the mountains, which I will show you."*
*Genesis 22:1-2*

# *FATHER ABRAHAM*

There was absolutely no way that Sarah, with a mother's heart, could have known where Abraham was taking Isaac that morning. She would have done everything within her power to prevent Abraham from leaving.

I have found myself at many altars over the years. Some I created willingly, some I fell upon in desperation, and some I was placed upon, kicking, screaming, squawking, squealing, ranting, and raving.

One of my most memorable altar experiences wasn't even my own. It was my husband's. God and I were still not on the best of speaking terms. I depended on Gary to remain spiritually intact so that we would have access to the throne when it was needed. Sean was three years old when Gary decided to pull a Father Abraham in the hospital emergency room.

After many months of manageable seizure activity, Sean went into a status seizure again. This was a life-threatening seizure episode where the doctors could not stop the seizure for nearly an hour. They were not able to get IV access because every single place where they could put an intravenous line in was unsuccessful. Finally, they called a surgeon to perform a "cut down" into his arterial vein to medicate him and intubate him. It looked like we were losing him! We had been here many times with the same team fighting to save our son. I could see the sheer panic on every one of their faces. The shift in the atmosphere was overwhelming. I could smell it, taste it, hear it and feel it.

In that moment of raw, paralyzing fear, I looked over and saw my husband get down on his knees, lift his hands, open his mouth and begin to pray. I watched his lips move and I realized that he was telling God that he had surrendered our son, that he trusted Him with our child, and that if it was His will, He could take our baby. Father Abraham was marching up Mount Moriah with our son.

I hated him! I wanted him to shut up and get up off the floor! I started praying my own prayer, "NO! GOD, NO! DO NOT TAKE HIM!" I wasn't ready, I still didn't trust God. I couldn't…I wouldn't let go. The ferocity in which I held on was indescribable. As I was begging God to stop listening to my husband, the doors opened and the team from Children's Hospital walked in and began to immediately work on Sean. It was as if they were ushered in by the angels. The air about them was confident and powerful and we knew that they would rescue our son. Finally, Sean stopped seizing.

Breathing tube inserted - check.

Ventilator on - check.

Ambulance ride to CHOP - check.

We all knew the drill.

I did not see a ram in a thicket that day, but God spared my son. Father Gary Abraham, your faith is amazing!

# CHAPTER SEVEN

## I WANT _____

# I WANT _____

S ean began special education at the age of three. I will forever remember my first visit to the school. The principal met me at the door, greeted me in a cheerful manner, and began to show me around the facility. I immediately heard cries, screams, moans, and other sounds that I don't know how to describe. I looked into the rooms and saw small children. Some of them were sitting in chairs and others were lying on the floor. While some seemed content, most were in distress - hence the strange sounds.

Without warning, my emotions ransacked my composure and I began sobbing in the hallway. I just could not imagine my child spending his days in this environment. I didn't want him to be one of those children lying on the floor, crying. I didn't want him to sit in a cubicle and try to make sounds discernible enough to receive small pieces of candy, cookies and chips as rewards. I saw wheelchairs, walkers and special bicycles lined up against the wall and I wanted to run as fast and as far away from there as I could.

The principal was so kind. Apparently, she had seen this reaction before and was capable of consoling mothers as they lost their minds in her hallways. She escorted me to the school liaison's office where I was given tissues and water. She introduced me to the social worker and then asked me to sit with them and talk. I felt understanding coming from each of them, but not pity. I realized what a nice change it was to be understood rather than pitied.

As they began to reassure me that this was a common reaction, they offered explanations about what I had seen. The social worker then dumped a pile of plastic pictures onto the table. On the back of each picture were small Velcro dots. She handed me a thick plastic strip with three pieces of Velcro, with the corresponding words, "I Want _____" printed on it. Next, she reached into the pile of plastic pictures lying on the table and retrieved one of them.

Over the first piece of Velcro I held in my hand, she placed a picture of the letter, "I." Over the second piece of Velcro, she placed the word, "Want." She left the third piece of Velcro empty and then explained to me that this sentence, "I Want _____" is the most important sentence in the world to children with autism who are non-verbal, as they are able to communicate their wants and needs by selecting an appropriate picture. I was comforted by the passion in her voice and grateful for the assurance of hope she offered me.

Despite my shock and horror at the introduction of special education, Sean adapted valiantly. He thrived on the attention and structure. He loved school and looked forward to riding his little yellow bus each day. His gains were slight and only recognized by the observations of the most devoted among us. He learned to sit still in 30-second increments and we hoped that he would build up to sitting still for actual minute increments. He was intensely potty trained in 15-minute increments. He was cajoled, prompted, bribed, encouraged, enticed, incited, and urged to make sounds, follow instructions, and imitate appropriate behaviors.

One of my greatest blessings that came from this early education was the formation of a Mom's group. I attended several of the meetings for moms, which were held at the school, and found the collaboration extremely helpful. However, I needed more. I needed women not only to talk to and share resources with, but I needed someone to speak to the spiritual part of me that was so broken by this new life I was now living. I needed women to pray with.

Out of this need, I began hosting the More to Life Mom's group. We gathered around my kitchen table for our first meeting and completely fell in love with each other. Without words, eye contact was enough for us to connect on a level we didn't even know existed until we arrived there. We shared everything. Our hopes, disappointments, fears, and worst nightmares became topics of discussion, catalysts for prayer and a source of great grace for each of us. These women became my heart sisters. Their children were my children. Their hopes were the same as mine. We wanted healthy children.

Special education teachers became my heroes and direct care staff became my SUPERHEROES! From patient bus drivers to compassionate principals, the work they do is honorable. I would never have chosen this life for myself or my child, but these incredible human beings have chosen to live daily in the world of autism. Our Seany has been educated and cared for by the best. Each year his one on one staff member became his "school mommy." I never had to worry about abuse or neglect when he was in their presence because I knew they were angels watching over him. Thank you Miss Ruth, Francesca and Deb.

Sean never did master the "I WANT_____," sentence strip, but his strides are immeasurable. Every ounce of accomplishment for him is worth its weight in pure gold.

# CHAPTER EIGHT

## *HIDING PLACES*

# HIDING PLACES

During Sean's many hospital admissions, my husband re-
treated to the chapel to pray while I took myself to the
cafeteria to eat. It was there that I discovered the comfort
of carbohydrates. I have always had a love for cake, but it wasn't
until my son was diagnosed with the rare seizure disorder that
on multiple occasions nearly killed him, that I developed a life or
death need for cake.

I hid in food, Gary hid in ministry, and sometimes we shared our
hiding places. I knew, from the outside, that ministry looked better
to those who were observing. I tried to be spiritual and visit the
chapel, but I always ended up at the cafeteria. I'm quite certain that
Jesus would have filled the great big hole in my heart if I hadn't
already stuffed it with mashed potatoes and ice cream.

During one particular hospital stay, Gary was gone to the chapel
to pray, and Sean went into a status episode. Alone, I stood there
helpless as I watched doctors and nurses work to save his life. My
husband was paged repeatedly and returned just as I was removed
from the room so that they could intubate our son, paralyze him,
and place him on a ventilator. Gary, of course, was sorry to have
missed the trauma, but could not wait to tell me his ministry ad-
venture that occurred in the chapel and how he was certain that

God was here with us.

Gary proceeded to tell me this amazing story about how he saw another man praying in the chapel and how he walked over to the man, laid hands on him, and the man received the Holy Ghost. As Gary was sharing his story with me, all I could think was, "Good for him...Good for you. I'm sure God is so proud of you, but your son almost died in here and I was all alone! God was with you in the chapel, but He was not in the trauma room with Sean."

Gary often found opportunities to minister by praying with other families in the hospital. He would walk the halls, looking into the rooms and scanning the faces of those who so desperately needed God to heal and comfort them. He recognized the silent pleading in the swollen eyes of parents begging God to allow their children to live. No one ever refused prayer.

I remember the sound of agony. The little boy who was in the bed next to Sean had just returned from a surgical biopsy. He was lying on his belly, sleeping comfortably snuggled on his pillow, with his mother and father on either side of his bed. As the curtain was closed, we could hear the doctor giving the report to his parents that the tumor was malignant. I cannot describe the wail that resounded in that room and throughout the entire floor, as his mother absorbed the blow of a cancer diagnosis. Gary and I held each other, weeping for them and feeling the pain of her wailing cries.

What I remember most about those hospital stays was feeling completely alone. It was not because people were not physically present. People were there. My husband was there and our parents came often. Family and friends called us on the phone to offer support, but no matter what comforting words they offered, I was alone. I had closed myself off and completely shut down.

For many years, I was angry at people for not visiting us. No cards,

flowers or balloons ever arrived. Today I understand why so many
of our family, friends, brothers and sisters did nothing, and I regret
not inviting them to share our pain, or welcoming them to help carry some of the load. I needed them desperately, and I needed God,
but my heart had turned to stone. How could anyone have known?
I always looked like I was okay. For every ambulance ride, ER visit,
and hospital admission, my hair was up and my clothes matched.
No matter what happened around me, I was calm, composed, and
cooperative. My attitude displayed great faith, my mouth uttered
appropriate prayers, and my life emanated inspiration. There is no
way anyone could have known the agony that raged inside of me.

After years of hiding myself in food, I developed an indescribable
amount of shame. Feelings of self–loathing became my best friend
as the cyclical Merry-Go-Round spun in dizzying circles, carrying
my hatred-hope-failure-hatred-hope-failure-hatred-hope-failure.
Round and round, over and over it continued, until I was lugging
around 100 excess pounds of disgusting, dimpled fat. I was miserable, lonely and so ashamed of the woman I saw in the mirror. I
knew that I had to change, but did not know how.

# CHAPTER NINE

## *CALL ME BART*

*"When Bartimaeus heard that Jesus of Nazareth was nearby, he began to shout, 'Jesus, thou Son of David, have mercy on me!' 'Be quiet!' many of the people yelled at him. But he only shouted louder, 'Son of David, have mercy on me!'" Mark 10:47–48*

# CALL ME BART

I t was time for my annual doctor visit, so I went to meet with Dr. Z. She greeted me with her usual smiles and pleasantries. She had not seen me since Sean's diagnosis, and when she inquired as to his wellbeing, I inappropriately started sobbing. She listened sympathetically, gently held my hand, and patted my back as I told her the woeful tale of his recent loss of language, continuation of his seizures and the increased amount of aggression and withdrawal from our world. When I finished speaking, dried my eyes and blew my nose, she dutifully handed me a script for Prozac and the business card of a psychiatrist she recommended that I talk to.

I left her office with a sense of hope. I had a secret weapon in my purse - a backup plan. After all, I had been praying for God to help me cope with my grief, but He was not doing a good job, as far as I was concerned. I was willing to give him a few more days, though. It was Friday when I saw the doctor and I told the Lord that I would not fill the prescription or call the psychiatrist until Monday. I gave Him until Sunday at midnight to fix me.

As I prepared for church on Sunday morning, my expectations were very low and dropping by the minute as I attempted to get the kids dressed and ready to go. Church had become such a chore. It was an emotional and physical endurance test for me twice a week. My husband was the co-pastor, I was the ladies' leader, and together we served as youth leaders. We had serious roles and responsibilities to fulfill. Ministry was our life and church was vital, but Sean hated church.

Everything about church was diametrically oppositional to an autistic child's sensory needs. The music was too loud for him, the people were unpredictable, and everyone hugged and touched when they said, "Praise the Lord." The services were long. Worship service lasted one hour, preaching lasted one hour, and the closing usually lasted one hour.

Sean was unable to sit still for five minutes, let alone three hours. I would hold him in my lap, wrestling for a while. Then I would put him down and chase him. Then I would take him into a vacant room and occupy him with snacks. This was how we did church. It was absolutely exhausting!

I asked and sometimes even pleaded for help. Occasionally, a sweet sister would attempt to help me, but it never turned out well or lasted very long. Sean would cry, scream, kick, smack and pinch them. Then he would take off running at full speed through the sanctuary or he would try to escape through the front door onto the street. Sometimes he would have a seizure.

People wanted to help, but they just didn't know how. I also didn't know how to be helped. When I suggested the formation of nursery staff, one special gal reminded me that I should not expect people to drop their lives in order to pick up mine. Week after exhausting week, I held onto my life all alone.

On this particular Sunday, I was desperately hoping that things would change. I brought the Prozac script and the psychiatrist's business card with me to offer before the Lord. I knew I was at the end of my rope. I had not had a breakthrough in a long time. I had cried and prayed a lot, but I had not had an altar experience for months. I needed time at the altar!

The service was particularly Pentecostal this Sunday. They were having a blow out, Holy-Rollin' service. Gary was on the platform, jumping up and down. Other brothers and sisters were hooping, hollering, running and worshipping everywhere, and in every way.

Sean and I were on the back row, wrestling, and I began to contemplate my options. I knew I'd had enough of this. I wanted out. As soon as I could reach in and grab my purse that Sister So and So (who was slain in the Spirit) was lying on top of, we were leaving and never coming back.

I finally saw her stir, and I made my move. Grabbing my purse and Sean's diaper bag, I started down the hallway. I was a few feet out of the sanctuary when I heard my name being called from the platform. "Sister Denise, please come to the front of the church. We want to pray for you."

"You've got to be kidding me! I am done with this!" I thought.

I obediently turned around and made my way to the front of the sanctuary thinking, "Okay, let's get this over with." To my surprise, the entire congregation seemed to come out of their seats and move in behind me, coming forward in support. The pastor started saying how much I meant to everyone and how much I was loved. I began to drop my negative attitude and my defenses. Then the tears came. Crying turned to sobbing, and then to wailing. I began to cry out with all my strength, "Jesus, JESUS!!!" Louder and louder, in sheer desperation and agony, I called on the name of the Lord. I finally dropped to my knees in complete and total surrender as I felt His presence.

Having been spiritually blinded by my painful circumstances, I could not see the only One who could help me. Jesus heard my cry and came to rescue me. I made it to the altar and He healed me there.

I believe therapy is helpful and medications are necessary at times to stabilize chemicals in the brain, but I had no need to fill my Prozac script or call the psychiatrist after that day.

# CHAPTER TEN

## *MY OTHER BOY*

# MY OTHER BOY

aron has been the ideal child and special in every way, except for the ways in which classify his brother as "special." He was an amazingly sweet baby who met every milestone (whether big or small) with smiles, giggles and joyous victories. From crawling, walking, talking, reading and writing, to everything else a child is supposed to learn, he mastered it all with ease.

Days turned into years as I watched him with pride and joy, grow into a smart, compassionate, funny, handsome and truly beautiful human being. He has been loving and loyal to his brother. Aaron has been a caregiver to Sean all of his life. He has changed his diapers, wiped food from his face, and dressed him for church many a Sunday to help mom. He has always been there for all of us.

I think back to those early years of his childhood when the ambulances would come and take his brother away. Mom and dad would leave him at grandma's house for days at a time, and he was fortunate to have loving grandparents who were always happy to care for him. I know that he enjoyed his time with them immensely. They lavished him with attention, watching his favorite Disney movies with him and feeding him healthy meals and sweet treats, attempting to fill the void of his family's absence.

I remember his little 4-year-old voice asking me, "Is Sean gonna die mommy?" To my horror, he then admitted, "I want him to die so you can always be with me." Oh, how it hurt to hear those words. I know he too, was still just a baby and only knew that he wanted his mommy. I felt such guilt for having left him so many times. Even the best care from mom-mom and pop-pop could not replace the love and attention he needed from me. Aaron did not have the security that a stable home life grants a child.

I can't help but wonder what effects this "special" upbringing will have on Aaron's life. There have been times during his teen years when he seemed to resent the constant demands of Sean. He would withdraw to his room or spend hours at his best buddy, Kyle's, house, where he could be free of weird noises and diaper duty. He loved being with a "normal" family and enjoyed the respite from our autistically-affected home. I am grateful that he had this point of refuge, where this family lovingly provided my son with hope and instilled a renewed faith for his future.

No one knows what the future will hold for my other boy, Aaron, my precious, gentle son who is so sensitive to the needs of others. I have no doubt that God planned his life perfectly and exactly as it is meant to be, including his brother. Perhaps one day, he will see the blessing and realize that he is a better human being, not in spite of, but because of, his love for Sean.

*To Aaron's Future Wife,*

*We have not met yet. I do not know your name or where you are from. I am pretty sure that your hair is brown. You are witty and sweet with a touch of bossiness and a gifted sense of fashion. You are intelligent, maybe quirky, and sensitive. You are a good church girl, faithful, prayerful and kind. You are a true Christian, loving and loyal to your family, friends and fellow humans. You are completely in love with Jesus and this amazing young man, Aaron.*

*Welcome to the Wynn clan. Surely, you have been warned that our family is different and hopefully you have considered the challenges you will face as you become a part of us. Aaron's only brother is profoundly affected by autism and so are our lives. You may not notice the effects on you personally or on your marriage for many years, but I know you will someday.*

*I promise to be a fantastic mother-in-law. God gave me two boys and although I couldn't love them an ounce more, I have longed for a daughter to share life with. I look forward to many happy times together. You can count on me to be there for you no matter the need. I will do my best for you.*

*I intend to live a long and healthy life or meet Jesus in the air when the trumpet sounds, but if God chooses an alternate route for me, I am going to need you. If I go insane, or get dementia or die, I am really going to depend on you to be here for my boys—both of them.*

*I pray that you have a great big love-filled heart and a resilient sense of humor.*

*Please take care of them for me.*

*Love,*
*Mom*

## CHAPTER ELEVEN

## *POOP, PAINT AND OTHER MESSES*

# POOP, PAINT AND OTHER MESSES

The most common messes occur with pee. Yes, I am talking about that bodily function. Sean wears diapers. He has been on a potty training schedule since he was two years old, but he still hasn't mastered the skill. Somehow, he fills his diapers beyond their capacity and they always leak. He also wets through his pajamas and bedding at night, then he comes to my bed where he wets through his new pajamas and my bedding. We have lots of laundry from the pee pee messes.

Then we have the next bodily fluid mess: blood. Sean does this fake sneeze thing that eventually leads to a nosebleed. I faint at the sight of blood, so these messes are difficult for me to clean up on my own. Gary usually cleans up the nosebleeds. Sean also has a problem with allowing bug bites or wounds to heal. He will pick the scabs until they bleed. He will pull out stitches and open surgical incisions, and yes, they bleed. And yes, I have fainted. Poor Gary often takes care of me and Sean at the same time.

The night Sean had surgery to replace his Vagal Nerve Stimulator (VNS) battery, I found him in the kitchen. He had opened the four-inch incision in his chest by scratching and pulling it, as evidenced by the blood on his fingers. I took a deep breath and hollered for Gary. He came running, panic-stricken, hyper alert, stumbling, and dizzy from being awoken in the middle of the night by my scream. As he began to take care of Sean, I made my way down the hall, intending to get the phone and call the doctor for advice. I remember the room spinning and sitting on the edge of my bed. Gary said that he heard a loud thump and knew immediately that I had passed out. I woke up on the floor with Gary staring down at me with pity and amusement, holding Sean's bloody hand.

Out of all the bodily fluid messes, however, it is the poop that does me in completely. I don't know what it is, but poop sends me over the edge. I am okay if poop is contained to the hiney or the toilet, but when it spreads to the walls and floors, I'm losing it.

One morning while doing housework, I had left Sean alone in his room, watching a video and playing with puzzle pieces on his bedroom floor. During my absence, he had a huge bowel movement and removed his diaper. He then stepped repeatedly in the poop as he walked all over his bedroom. When I returned to check on him, I opened his door to see hundreds of poop foot prints all over the floor and a smell that cannot be described.

I knew that I was going to snap, so I called my husband as quickly as I could, before my screams took over. I don't know what he heard in my voice, but he was home in minutes and he must have taken Sean somewhere - probably to my mom's (my parents are faithful first responders to all of our drama). I don't know where he was, but he was gone.

I vaguely remember being on my hands and knees, surrounded by buckets of water, soap and towels. I was loudly wailing these weird moaning cries as I scrubbed, losing my mind with each wringing of the poop-filled rags.

After I had done my best to clean the disgusting mess, I filled my bathtub, climbed in, put my head under the water, and never wanted to get out. Gary came in and told me that his mom was on her way over to help clean up the mess. Then he handed me the phone. He had called Cindy, my best friend and therapist. She said, "Hey, whatcha doin?" Her usual opening to every conversation we've had on the phone for almost 20 years.

"I'm in the bathtub planning to drown myself," I replied. Then I laughed, because only she can make me laugh at nothing, at every-thing.

"I'm coming over to help with the poop," she said.

"No need." I said. "My mother-in-law is on the way."

Cindy was relieved, I'm sure. "So, how about we get you some fresh air, Buddy?"

Yes, that was just what I needed. Knowing that my husband, my par-ents, my in-laws and my dear best friend were all there for me, got me out of the bathtub and back to sanity one more time.

I sat with Cindy on a bench outside of Applebee's restaurant and laid my head on her shoulder for as long as I needed, not caring how crazy it may have looked to others. I felt completely grateful that I had not actually gone crazy. That was a close one!

After these experiences with poop, you would think that cleaning up emptied jars of splattered pickle relish would be a cinch. Well, no. My boy has created messes that I have had to stand back, calculate, and then plan the possible options for cleanup. Some of these include Ranch dressing on the walls, hand soap on the ceiling, body lotion on the windows, and a gallon of milk spreading across the floor and dripping down into the heating vents. Sean has an infatuation with empty bottles and whatever contents are in said bottle must always be removed by dumping and shaking until he is satisfied that it is empty. Then he goes on a quest, looking for the next bottle.

Sean has never been a good sleeper and somehow finds ways to occupy himself throughout the night. On one such night, he located a box of Crayola finger paint in bottles. He emptied every bottle and every color, creating an amazing psychedelic graphic design all over his bedroom. The walls, the floor, the furniture, the bedding, the curtains and yes his body, head to toe, were all covered in yellow, blue, red, purple and green paint. Gary grabbed the video camera and began filming Sean and the disaster he had created. He started laughing at Sean's oblivious pleasure and the ridiculousness of it all. I tried to find laughter as I attempted to fathom some way to clean up the disaster, but I could not.

We filed an insurance claim, threw away all the damaged furnishings, and repainted the room. Later, we received an insurance check for $1,700.00 to cover the cost of repairs. I do distinctly remember smiling when this check arrived and I have laughed many times when retelling this story.

# CHAPTER TWELVE

## BUMPS, BRUISES, AND BROKEN BONES

*"Lord, have mercy on my son: for he is epileptic, and is very ill: for often he falls into the fire, and often into the water." Matthew 17:15*

—◆◆◆—

# BUMPS, BRUISES, AND
# BROKEN BONES

Life with a seizure disorder is unpredictable at best and traumatic at worst. I am convinced that I suffer a form of Post
Traumatic Stress Disorder (PTSD) caused by some of the
worst seizures we have experienced. Any sign of a twitch, a strange
groan, a stumble or a quick movement can send me into panic mode.
My son has had seizures everywhere you can imagine: in the car, in
the bathtub, at school, at church, on the bus, while walking, sitting,
standing, sleeping, and swimming. You name it. We have had a seizure there while doing that. There have been cuts, sprains, broken
bones, black eyes, bruises, and even a second degree burn.

More often than not, thank God, his seizures do not harm him, but
we have had some doozies. The first major injury was caused by a
seizure on rocks in a parking lot at the park, which required a visit
to the emergency room and ten stitches over his right eyebrow. This
prompted us to consider the importance of protecting his head and
face from future injuries, so I ordered a foam helmet from a Special
Needs catalog.

The day the helmet arrived was a sad day for me. Unwillingly, I was
admitting that this seizure disorder would be a part of our daily existence. The scary, ugly and dangerous twitching, shaking, and falling
over was here to stay and we had to protect Sean's head. The only

funny thing about this helmet was that Sean looked just like Elmer Fudd when we put it on his head. "Shhh, I'm hunting wabbits!!" I laughed until I cried. And then I just cried.

No more head injuries occurred except for the one time we neglected to put the helmet on Sean because we were walking with him. He had become restless during a church service at junior high camp, so we took him outside to walk around the campground. We both let go of Sean for a few seconds and Sean got ahead of us and down he went on his face into the pavement. Another emergency room visit ensued, but miraculously there were no broken bones, missing teeth or stitches. The bruising, however, was horrid! Both of his eyes were swollen shut and his face was black and blue for weeks. You can be assured from that moment, these words resounded in my head: "Helmet - ON!!!"

With his head and face protected, we now have only limbs and all other body parts to worry about. He has broken toes and fingers and his right arm. The broken arm never even fazed him, except that he wanted the cast off. His pain tolerance is unbelievable. He still attempted to carry heavy items, such as a full gallon of milk, with that broken arm. He used his plaster-wrapped arm for the entire eight weeks and sometimes used it as a weapon, whacking us good.

One Sunday morning while preparing for church, I left the ironing board and iron unattended for a moment. We heard a crash and a load moan and then my screams filled the room as we saw Sean lying on the floor seizing, with the hot iron between the crook of his arm. That one required an ambulance ride and weeks of burn treatments.

There is no way that I can adequately describe the bumps and bruises my boy has endured, or the pain and injury he has handled with the courage of a ninja warrior. There were many moments where the seeming injustice of his injuries angered me. The seizure disorder sickens me completely, but I know that he has a brain malformation which causes the epilepsy, so I accept the occurrence of seizures. The injuries, however, seem senseless. Spiritually and emotionally in my mommy mind, I don't understand why an innocent child has to suffer.

One particular night, I was feeling quite pitiful. It was almost midnight. I was recounting a horrible week of seizure activity, when I felt The Lord prompt my spirit to watch the movie, The Passion of the Christ. I didn't want to watch the movie. It was late. The movie is long, and watching it once was difficult enough for me. I couldn't even watch the whipping scene.

I tried to ignore the prompting as I made my way down the hallway to go to bed. Again, I felt prompted to watch the movie. More specifically, The Lord asked me to watch that dreaded whipping scene.

"Okay, I know God is serious about this," I said to myself. I found the DVD and put it in the player. As the movie began, I fast forwarded through most of it and then stopped at a scene with Mary. I felt God say, "Watch this from a mother's perspective."

So I did.

I watched Mary's son as he was dragged into the courtyard, taunted, teased, smacked, whipped and beaten beyond recognition. I saw Mary's innocent boy's flesh torn apart as his blood spilled on the ground, and I thought, "God forgive me! There is absolutely nothing in my life this messy, this painful, or this unjust!"

As Mary knelt in the courtyard and began to wipe His blood from the ground, I felt her anguish. I could hear her thinking, "Why have they done this to you, my innocent boy?" Not understanding why and not knowing whether her son was dead or alive, Mary continued to wipe His blood from the stone pavement, knowing His blood was too precious to lay on the ground, and too sacred for one drop to be wasted.

I realize this is not an actual Biblical account recorded in the gospel, but my emotional understanding of what was depicted in this scene was this: I don't know why they have beaten you, why you have been taken away, or why your blood has been spilled, but I will not allow any of it to be wasted!

Mary amazed me. How did she not run through the streets, screaming like a mad woman? How did she sit at His feet as he hung on the cross and not act like a crazy mom? I would have been stomping around at the foot of the cross, hollering up at Jesus to get down from there! I would have demanded that He speak one word and change it all, like He had done so many times before. I would have asked Him to summon a thousand-angel army to rush in and tear that city up! But Mary did none of that. She just sat there weeping and waiting for what would come, trusting God completely.

Mary's type of trust was different than my type of trust. I just knew God would do it my way and make it all better for me. Mary trusted Him unconditionally, no matter how, what, or why.

As I watched the scenes of this movie from a mother's perspective, I pleaded with God to forgive me. Then, my prayers shifted to a place of surrender. I asked God to show me how to trust Him completely with Sean. I asked Him to help me not to waste the anguish, the pain, and the suffering, but to somehow give it purpose, power and meaning.

# CHAPTER THIRTEEN

## *TALKING HANDS*

## *TALKING HANDS*

When Sean lost the ability to communicate with words, he began to use his hands to talk. No, he did not learn sign language to communicate his needs. Rather, he communicated by hitting, smacking, pinching, pulling and punching.

A smack and a pinch from a two-year-old child is annoying, but as the child grows, the force of the blows and the result of the physical contact worsens significantly. We waited too long to deal with this behavior. We were so consumed with seizures and learning how to live with autism, that we gave into the annoying pinches and smacks. Sean learned that he would get what he wanted if he beat on us long enough.

The aggression became a constant source of stress on the family. Our support system diminished as caregivers resigned from helping, due to the abuse they received while trying to care for Sean. Every one of our friends and family members that has spent time with him has either a scar or a distinct memory of a good smack they received from his talking hands.

Some days were unbearable. Eight hours can feel like eighty hours when you are enduring constant physical altercations. The worst days were experienced when the school was closed. Sean loved school and his routine was the most critical component of each day. When the school bus ran late, his entire day would be "off" and the aggression would increase. When school was closed, his entire day would be "way off" and the aggression was intolerable. Summer vacation was an annual nightmare of eighty hour days, sleepless nights, and endless beatings. Holiday breaks were dreaded and never celebrated, because we all knew what to expect.

Over the years, Sean perfected his pinch-and-pull technique to the point where skin would be removed in long chunks from our hands, arms and faces. He also learned new ways to use his enormous strength by head-butting and kicking us. As he grew into his 6-foot, 190 pound frame, there were blows that I thought would kill me. Aaron and Gary took many beatings, always trying to protect me, the one whom Sean seemed to both love and abuse the most. Gary would wrap his arms around me to deflect the scratches from my body to his. Aaron would attempt to distract his brother with movies or remove him from the room for "time-out." This behavior was completely beyond our skill set. Nothing worked to decrease the aggression. We tried everything from behavior modification to medication. Nothing worked.

Driving Sean in the car became a serious risk. He loved car rides, but would become aggressive if I passed a fast food restaurant without stopping to get food. He would begin saying, "eat, EAT," as he pulled my hair, pinched my arms and pinch-pulled my shoulder from the back seat. After enduring repeated kicks to the head one day, we finally purchased a minivan with a third seat where Sean could sit without reaching the driver's seat.

The hand talking was excruciating to live with, but living with it was our only choice. It seemed that no one had any answers. Improvisation became our source of existence. Day in and day out we managed the best we could. We were grateful for the help of family and friends on weekends and school breaks, but we were so sorry for the abuse they endured.

My mom would always say, "He was no trouble at all," while dad stood by with Band-Aids all over his wounded arms. Rachel learned to wear long sleeves when baby sitting, and Nancy made him fold laundry to busy those heavy hands. Then she would run circles around the house to avoid Sean's painful smacks. Paid home health aides lectured us on how to be better parents and quit accepting assignments at the Wynn residence.

Dr. Dave was the first to suggest we consider residential placement. During a routine wellness visit at the pediatrician's office, Sean tried to remove items from the vaccine refrigerator. "Juice!!" he kept saying, as he pulled the door open and emptied bottles from the shelves. After the removal of Sean from the room by five staff members, a hefty kick to Dr. Dave's jaw, and a wrestling match in the hallway, we finally got him outside and into the van. Once the van door closed, Dr. Dave placed his arm around my shoulder and told me that it was time to consider Sean's future. He said, "You have lived like this for so long, that you don't even know what a normal life is. You can't live like this." He urged me to begin making arrangements right then and not to wait until everything was broken. I remember my exact words, "I cannot think about letting him go until every day hurts as bad as that thought."

I could not begin to think of life without Sean. As bad as it was, I was not ready to let go of my crazy, difficult world. But I felt it getting closer.

## CHAPTER FOURTEEN

## *AND THE RAIN, RAIN, RAIN CAME DOWN, DOWN, DOWN*

# AND THE RAIN, RAIN, RAIN CAME DOWN, DOWN, DOWN

S ean had a seizure while walking from the front door of our home to the school bus in our driveway. He laid on the cold, wet sidewalk until help arrived. He is too big now for me to move him, so I sat on the damp concrete next to my 190 pound baby, waiting for him to wake up, and wiping the blood from his hands where his knuckles had scraped the pavement during his fall. I looked up and asked God if He could see us sitting there. There was no answer from above, but I knew He was watching. I let a few tears race down my cheeks, and then choked the rest back, like I've learned to do. I got up to get my cell phone so I could call my husband. There was no answer.

Then it started to rain.

I ran inside and grabbed some blankets and tried calling Gary again. Still no answer. I tried to wake Sean, but he was unresponsive. He was shivering and turning a pasty, pale shade of blue. I dialed the all too familiar 9-1-1 phone number. As we waited, I wedged myself under his upper body, lifted his head onto my lap, covered him with blankets, and shielded him from the rain with my body. I looked at my boy, still unconscious, his face and hair soaked from the rain, and then once again, looked up to the sky. This time I did not ask God if He could see us. I began screaming at Him, demanding, that

He look at us.

"Look at us! Look! Why don't you care?" There was no answer, except for the pitter patter of the rain and the approaching sirens in the distance.

The police arrived first and then the ambulance. Sirens and all, they made their way down our long driveway. They greeted us with pitiful familiarity. We had all met before. It had been fourteen years of intermittent scenes just like this one. They all varied, according to the length of the seizure or the injuries that resulted from the impact of his body hitting the ground. With or without warning, at least once a week, there is a seizure.

If only it were just the seizures or just the autism, but the combination of the two creates a life that is far from manageable.

I've always said I wouldn't let Sean go until life hurt more than the thought of letting him go. Life really hurt right then. I've been angry. I've been sad. I've been numb. I've been cold. I've experienced every emotion a human being is capable of feeling. I didn't even know the name for what I felt in that moment.

Maybe a combination of all of those feelings interwove themselves inside my spirit, choking me and squeezing the air from my lungs. Involuntary deep breaths escaped and saved me from suffocating.

I felt like Winnie the Pooh and Piglet must have felt as they were carried away by raging currents in the scene from the classic story, "Winnie the Pooh and the Blustery Day." Snatches of the song played over and over in my head, in almost a mocking way:

> *And the rain, rain, rain*
> *came down, down, down*
> *in rushing mighty rivulets...*

Washed away in the deluge, as was I, all my hope for healing and normalcy, all my determination to keep our family together, and all my reservations of letting go, washed away in the rain that day.
It was time to find help.

# CHAPTER FIFTEEN

## LETTING GO

*When God Says No*

# LETTING GO

I had placed Sean on the altar and then taken him back off more times than I could count. Today it's your will, God. Tomorrow, I have a better idea. Let me just handle it myself. I don't like how you are handling this, God."

I sat at a Ladies Conference at the Chapel in Willow Valley, listening to Diana Reed speak to us. Her story did not have a happy ending, and for the first time, I began to wonder if I was hoping, expecting, and believing God for a miracle that was not part of His plan. I asked my soul, "What if God never heals Sean?" I remember kneeling down and uttering, "Not my will, but your will, God. I accept your will."

I had finally surrendered.

You would think that making the decision to let go would be the hardest part, because it hurt like no pain I had ever experienced. There is no way to describe the feelings that accompany choosing to allow your child to go away and be cared for by complete strangers.

We began to look at our options and soon realized that we only had two: (1) crisis placement, or (2) keeping him at home. We were told that Sean would need to be admitted to a crisis facility first before he could obtain a residential placement.

There were only three crisis facilities for children. Bancroft in Haddonfield, New Jersey, was close to home, but we were erroneously led to believe that, due to funding, this facility was not an option for us. Johns Hopkins in Baltimore, Maryland was three hours from home and accepted insurance, but the waiting list was two years long and based on urgency rather than chronological order. Then there was Cumberland Hospital for Children in Cumberland, Virginia. It was five hours away from home. We knew it would be horrible. We knew it would be the most difficult thing we had ever done and I did not know if I would survive it without a complete nervous breakdown. However, there was no other way to get the help we needed for Sean and for our family.

The day I decided that residential placement was the best decision for our family, I fell to the floor. I could not pray. I just kept saying, "God, you know..." The scripture stirred inside me that day was, "This light affliction worketh an eternal weight of glory." Surrender. Come on, Isaac. Let's get you back on the altar. Mommy's trusting God today. What a coincidence that these experiences occurred only when I got to the end of myself, and not a second beforehand. Self-sufficiency is such a trap.

I will never forget Sean's last night at home. I gave him a haircut and groomed his hands and feet. He took a long bubble bath in my great big Jacuzzi. I remember the extra care I took as I performed each part of our nightly bedtime routine. I gave him his medication, made his snack, and brushed his teeth. I began to cry, knowing that this would be the last time I would put his jammies on, tuck him into his bed, and kiss him goodnight.

"Oh, GOD, how will I survive this?"

Before retiring to bed, Gary and I went into Sean's room to pray. He had already fallen asleep. He was completely at peace and unaware that his mommy and daddy would wake him at 4 a.m., drive him five hours away from home, and leave him in a strange place with strange people. I climbed onto one side of his bed, Gary on the other, and Aaron laid across the foot of the bed. Surrounding our forever baby, we began to sob and weep as we prayed for his safety, his care, his heart and ours. I felt anguish, dread, fear, panic, sorrow, deep sorrow, the sorrow of death.

We held each other a long time, sobbing. When Gary finally looked at me, he said, "I can't lose both of you." He left the room and made a phone call. When he returned, he told me that he did not want me to go to Virginia in the morning and that our friend, Steven D'Amico, was going with him. We had known Stevie since he was a little guy. We went to church together and knew and loved his family for years, including his sister, Angela, who has Downs Syndrome. Stevie understood what we were feeling. Grateful that his sweet sister has remained at home with their family, he offered us his strength and optimism.

I made sure Sean's bags were packed and ready, took a sleep aid and went to bed. I awoke to silence. I walked down the hall to Sean's room. I climbed into his bed, taking in the smell of his scent on the pillow, and wept until I had nothing left. I got up, made the bed and closed the door. I would not open that door again for a long time.

Gary returned home that evening, looking like he had aged ten years. He tried to tell me that he was okay and that Sean was fine, but both were lies. Gary's health began to decline rapidly as symptoms of Crohn's Disease emerged. He also began suffering with muscle spasms and debilitating lower back problems. Despite all of that, though, he pushed on, forcing himself daily to get out of bed and into the world where the busyness kept him from completely falling apart.

Through it all, we made that long drive to Virginia every other weekend for more than a year. We pastored our church. We worked our full time jobs. We grieved for our boy. No, Sean did not die, but our dreams for him died. Our hope for his healing died. Our faith in God died.

Every visit broke our hearts more than we thought possible. How does a broken heart keep breaking? How many fragmented pieces can it hold?

Sean's weight dropped from 190 pounds to 134 pounds. He was skeletal. He had scratches and bruises. He hid his eyes from us, covering them with both of his hands, unwilling to look at us, sometimes for hours during our visits. We were losing him!

I cannot describe the fear, the doubt, the regret, sorrow and the suffocating guilt I felt each time we drove away, leaving him there. I wanted to take him home with us. I wanted my baby back. I wanted to take him off of the altar. God was not going to provide a ram for us and I was going to lose my son. Everything in me wanted to pull him off the altar again, but I couldn't. This time I couldn't. I did not know what I would do with him. How could I handle life with Sean without God? I needed God! I had to let go. I had to trust Him.

# CHAPTER SIXTEEN

## THE VISION

# THE VISION

It was a Monday morning. I was driving to work when I received a call from a pastor's wife. I knew her, but not very well. The little I did know was that she was a prayer warrior. She told me that she was having a ladies' prayer meeting in her home that morning and felt impressed by God to call and ask me if I had a need. I briefly told her of our need to bring Sean home from Virginia. I then asked her to pray for a placement in New Jersey, close to our home.

Later that evening, she called me and said that she had been wrestling with her thoughts that entire day, as to whether or not to tell me what had occurred at the prayer meeting. She finally gave into the prompting of the Holy Ghost and described a vision that one of the ladies had while they were praying for Sean. She described a scene in an elaborate office. It was a professional building with large wooden desks and ornate wood trim work on the walls. She saw a women dressed in a suit, sitting behind a desk and speaking with an elegantly dressed couple. She heard a small part of a conversation regarding the couple moving and taking their child out of state with them. The lady did not understand this vision or the words she heard, but she said that somehow she knew that the child's leaving would provide a placement for Sean.

As she told me this vision, I began to weep. Although the vision made no sense to me either, I felt a confirmation in my spirit that she was telling me something very important and something very true. The only residential placement appropriate for Sean, which was close to home, was Bancroft. It is the best in the state, but it does not have any elaborate office space or real wood or people dressed in suits.

Time went on and our sad, exhausting trips to Virginia continued. One day while working, my husband met at woman who had a son with Autism. They talked for a long time. Her story was so similar to ours. She told him about her experience with her son and that she had hired a lawyer at a cost of $30,000, to gain placement in a residential facility in New Jersey.

When Gary told me about their conversation, I felt hope rising in me. Every time I heard the words, "residential placement," I thought of the vision. I knew that we did not have $30,000, but I was certain we had to hire a lawyer.

Finally, through a friend of a friend, we were given the name of the lawyer in North Jersey who specializes in disability law. I called, made the appointment, and in three weeks we went to meet her at her office near New York City. When we located the address and pulled into the lot, I looked up at a huge office building. As we entered the building, I noticed the professional décor. Dark, rich, ornate wood was everywhere.

After exiting the elevator, we walked the length of that long hallway, looking into offices with large wooden desks. Behind those desks sat people wearing suits. In the most elaborate office space of all, we met Lisa Parles, Esquire. I knew that this was a scene from the vision. This was God answering our prayers!

She listened to our story and then explained the typical procedure to us for securing placement for a child with autism. It was complicated and expensive. She knew professionally and personally how difficult the process was. She too had a son with autism. Our hearts connected and Gary and I knew that she would do her best for us.

She told us that she had another family looking at Bancroft and that the placements were not only very limited, but they were also few and far between. We gave her a retainer fee of $3,600 and she began to research the funding options we would need before we could even be considered for the Bancroft waiting list.

Residential placement costs approximately $150,000 per year. Typically, the cost is shared by the school district and a government agency such as Division of Developmental Disabilities (DDD). Sean had been on the DDD placement list for funding for many years. He was number 3,091 on the list. While researching the funding options, our lawyer found a funding program called, "Return to New Jersey," that Sean would be eligible for because he had been placed out of state. She secured the funding and we waited for a place to open.

Several weeks passed and then the call came.

"Mrs. Wynn, I have great news. Earlier today, I met with a couple who informed me that they would be moving out of New Jersey and have decided against placing their child at Bancroft. The placement is open and I will advocate for Sean to have it."

She made the calls, the appointments, did the paperwork, and within the month, had secured Sean's placement at Bancroft. We then made our happiest trip to Virginia to go get our boy.

---

*Write the vision, make it plain on tablets, that he may run who reads it,*
*for the vision is yet for an appointed time, but at the end it will speak,*

*and it will not lie, though it tarries, wait for it, because it will surely come. Habakkuh 2:2*

⸺∞⸺

Sean transitioned beautifully to the Bancroft Campus and the staff has been kind, caring and loving. He enjoys school and his housemates. He recently moved into a community group home and is now able to visit us at home on the weekends. Our family has been healed and restored. Life is not perfect but it is very, very good.

# CHAPTER SEVENTEEN

## *FOR BETTER OR WORSE*

# FOR BETTER OR WORSE

On June 2, 1990, Gary and I stood before God, family, friends, and witnesses to make our wedding vows. We promised to love and cherish one another in sickness and in health, for richer or poorer, in good times and bad, for better or worse.

The statistics were not in our favor for maintaining this promise. The divorce rate is said to be 85% for couples who have a child with disabilities. The chronic stress on the marriage relationship, finances, and individual emotional depletion increases the likelihood of divorce.

We held our vows sacred and promised that divorce was never an option. However, emotional divorce was never discussed. I do not believe that we were aware of the term itself or the condition of our marriage when we experienced it. I only knew that I often felt far away and disconnected from him. I did not bother to ask him if he felt the same. We just lived our lives. We went to work, church and family gatherings. We ate together, slept together, and raised our boys.

Neither one of us is confrontational. We are awesome at avoiding arguments. Somehow, we were each programmed to appease, offer the benefit of the doubt, and extend grace to others. We are lovers, not fighters, but we had so much to fight for. We just didn't know how. I was always exhausted and too tired to talk, let alone argue. He was always good-natured, kind, and easily put off. We truly are a perfect pair.

The distance between us varied. There were times when we clung to each other for strength, stability and refuge. Our love held us. Then there were times of great loneliness, avoidance and resentment that kept us apart. Our vows held us.

Food was my companion and the effect it had on my body insulated me emotionally. My subconscious plan was most likely that my unattractive, rippled, dimpled fat would also insulate me physically, just so that I could be left alone. Just so that he would leave me and it would all be over and I could be completely miserable, without any hope, joy or pleasure. I did not care if the marriage ended. I did not care if my life ended. I can't say that I wanted to die, nor can I say that I didn't want to die. It was not the kind of "want to die" that makes you cut your wrist, overdose on pills, or drive into oncoming traffic, but it was the kind that wouldn't care if the oncoming traffic crashed into me. We have a train that passes our house, and more often than I want to admit, I did not even look before crossing the tracks.

Self-destructive behaviors became my hiding place. Food was first and then I discovered the great mind numbing comfort of shopping. It didn't take long for the debt to mount. The more I shopped, the more I hid the credit card bills, receipts, handbags, shoes and clothing.

Gary had his hiding places too. His hobbies were neither self-destructive nor expensive, yet our marriage suffered equally when he hid in his "acceptable" places. He enjoys hunting and outdoor sports. He remained extremely active with church and Bible studies. While pastoring, he answered every call, performed visitations, and offered his undivided attention to each member when they needed him. Because he was so busy, he didn't really notice the distance between us. We both have this incredible way of appearing to do the right thing even when we don't want to. Going through the motions kept us from feeling the cumulative effects of the distance on our marriage.

When we finally took the time to look at the distance between us, we knew that we had some work to do if we were going to make it. Gary began to feel the full weight of depression much later than I did. I numbed mine and he buried his. His emotional pain eroded his physical health as he experienced severe, debilitating back pain and symptoms of an autoimmune disease. For the first time in his life, he was not able to work. This caused a downward spiral in his body and soul. I started to worry about him. Pushing all of my emotions aside, I reached across the distance to be supportive. Without any hesitation, he reached back, and together we began to close the gap between us.

Gary attended physical therapy for his body and met with a Christian counselor for his soul. We realized that neglecting to honestly confront our disappointment and heartache, had caused each of us to stockpile our resentment. As we uncovered the underlying issues and truthfully admitted our struggles with our faith, healing came. Once Gary confessed his anger toward God, he was free to release the river of resentment that his heart had harbored for years.

We forgave one another for the selfish ways by which we had both attempted to grieve. I admitted my sins and he confessed his. God gave us indescribable grace through all of this, saving our marriage and our souls from destruction.

For better or worse, till death do us part.

# CHAPTER EIGHTEEN

# HEAVEN OR HEALING - WHAT DOES THE CHURCH BELIEVE?

# HEAVEN OR HEALING - WHAT DOES THE CHURCH BELIEVE?

What does the church believe about people with disabilities? Should they stand in lines and be anointed with oil until the healing comes? Should they accept their affliction and live by faith until it's time to go to Heaven? Or should they do both?

I seriously, and with honest, heart-wrenching desperation, hope that the severely and profoundly disabled have a free pass to Heaven. Whether this longing aligns with theology or Scripture is beyond my scope of knowledge, but my heart understands it perfectly.

I truly wish that I had answers. I would love to write a "how to" chapter and tell people, pastors, and fellow humans what needs to happen so that those with profound disabilities would thrive in our churches.

It is so sad that over fifty million Americans have some form of disability and very few of them will ever visit our churches. Look around your church on Sunday and see if it isn't so. Talk about a mission field! Those with disabilities and those who love them would fill our churches if we could figure out how to accommodate their needs with ministry.

One evening while sitting with a group of women, a pastor's wife began telling stories about how residents from a group home would visit their church. She laughed and said that she and her husband were afraid that they would become known as the Church of the Retarded Folks. A few others told stories of their experiences with the strange noises and behaviors. It sounded like they were talking about my boy, and in my mind, I smacked every one of them right in their laughing faces.

I probably should have told them about Kathy from Canada, who in desperation took her son, profoundly affected by Autism, into a church because she was starving for the presence of God. After the worship portion of the service ended, the quiet sanctuary was intermittently filled with her child's noises, and she was quickly asked to go into another room where "she and her son would be more comfortable." In tears, she left the building, feeling embarrassed, heartbroken and enraged. Kathy had not returned to a church until the night I met her at a Family Life Conference in Belleville, Ontario. Her son was now 27 years old and her marriage was failing. Still desperate for the presence of God, she received the Holy Ghost during that Sunday service. She began to attend church regularly where she and her son were welcomed with open arms into the sanctuary. Her mother began going to church with her too and her marriage was restored. Her husband sits beside her in that wonderful church every Sunday. When her son, Chris became ill, the church family surrounded them with prayer, words of encouragement, and acts of kindness. When their beautiful forever child passed away, the church was there to undergird them with love and support.

I should have told the group of laughing women about Kathy, or confessed my offense, but I was tired, and after all, everything they said was true. It just wasn't funny.

It is not funny when you are the one trying to keep your boy quiet with puzzles and cheerios, or trying to take your 6-foot-tall boy into the ladies' restroom. It is definitely not funny when trying to discreetly clean the pee-pee spot off of the pew because his diaper leaked. We know that we are a distraction! We know the sounds and behaviors are loud and strange! But where should we go? Where is our worship service? Where is our altar? Where is our sanctuary? Where do we go to hear God's Word preached? Where do we find fellowship, acceptance, and love?

Parents of children with chronic, serious, life-altering disabilities pray daily, and only sometimes, on purpose. In sheer desperation, I have made altars on bathroom floors, sidewalks, in my car, and while pacing hallways. These are the prayers that come without the ability to form thoughts and without the will to speak.

As it stands now, the only hope of Heaven for the severely disabled is a free pass because they do not fit into our churches. They are often ushered into empty fellowship halls, the empty Sunday school room at the very end of the corridor, or into an empty cry room. Empty rooms - a place where no one is disturbed and no one is uncomfortable.

I am not criticizing. I am not angry. Believe me. We pastored Cornerstone Christian Life Center for seven years and could not accommodate our son. We had sincere intentions of developing a Special Needs ministry. We held separate services for children and adults with cognitive disabilities but we never could figure out how to make church work for Sean. He was brought to church by his caregiver and left when he had enough. He typically lasted two songs. Sad? Frustrated? Yes. There are no simple answers or 10 steps to success programs that will solve this problem.

The best experience and the closest we came to attending church as a family was at Calvary Tabernacle. Under the ministry of Stan and Cindy Miller, we found refuge and healing beyond imagination, as the church welcomed us with open hearts and open arms. Not only were we treated with dignity and respect, but Calvary Tabernacle also hired an outside caregiver to take care of Sean during the church services so that Gary and I could be restored. They arranged a group of "Sean's friends" to spend time caring for him during services and special events. This sanctuary was the starting point where I was finally able to grow in ministry, develop my spiritual gifts, and where I found a renewed love for the Word of God and prayer. I could finally trust God with my heart. I could finally trust people with my son. They loved him and cared for him as one of their own.

How can the church welcome those with disabilities? The answer is this: with love. Open your hearts, your doors and your financial support to include them in the church on the deepest level possible. Each one will be different. God knows how different, for it is He who made them. Love them like He does.

———⚬⚬———

*"And the king will answer and say unto them, Verily, I say unto you, Inasmuch as you have done it unto one of the least of these my brethren, ye have done it unto me." Matthew 25:40*

———⚬⚬———

———⊗⊗⊗———

This chapter is dedicated to
Christopher Peter Jones
In Loving Memory
1984 - 2013

———⊗⊗⊗———

# CHAPTER NINETEEN

## *THE FUTURE*

# THE FUTURE

I am amazed and ashamed at my propensity for avoidance. I avoid pain and discomfort. I also avoid pleasure and intimacy. How many Kit Kat's or Reese's cups must I consume before making a difficult phone call or responding to an upsetting email? How many cups of coffee must I drink before I have enough energy to fold the laundry? How many rows will I crochet or chapters will I read before spending time in my husband's arms? I would not label myself a procrastinator, not because the definition isn't suitable, but because I would rather not admit to possessing such a defective character trait.

I will admit that when the outcome is uncertain, the task is too great, or the cost is too high, I avoid it. When the risk goes beyond what I am willing to lose, I avoid it. When my only reason is that I just don't want to do it, I avoid it.

So how does one such as myself, prepare for the future? I do what I can and the rest is living by pure faith. Our last Living Will and Testament is complete. The plans have been made for Sean's future. The parts that we humans have control over have been arranged. Ultimately, I don't know much about the here and now, or about our future on this earth. I just pray that my precious boy is always cared for and loved. I hope that people are kind and compassionate to him. I never want him to be hungry, cold or lonely, to lie in a wet bed or sleep in a soiled diaper. I want people to care for him when I can't, to hold him when he needs reassurance and affection, and to kiss his sweet cheeks and tell him he is loved by a Great Big Wonderful God.

There are stories that haunt me. Tragic stories about abuse, neglect and death of the innocent. I read the pitiful confession of a man who knew that his autistic brother was being raped by a staff member while institutionalized, yet he did nothing about it because he didn't want to know. The news reported that a 20-year-old autistic man died after being forgotten in a hot van for five hours. A 14-year-old autistic boy drowned in a school swimming pool while his caregiver was distracted. These stories hurt me deeply. They sicken me, scare me and infuriate me. Depending on others to keep your child safe, secure, and alive is desperate blind faith. Depending on them to be kind, loving and caring is true faith - faith that knows without doubt that God is holding my whole world in His hands.

For now, I am living day by day, trusting the One who created all things and charges his angels to watch over my precious boy. I keep my eyes on the Eastern sky, listening for the sound of a trumpet blowing, and looking forward to the last time God says NO.

---

*"And God Himself shall wipe away every tear from their eyes and there shall be NO more death, NO more sorrow, NO more crying, and there shall be NO more pain, for the former things have passed away... Then He who sat on the Throne said, "Behold, I make all things new. And He said to Me...WRITE, FOR THESE WORDS ARE TRUE AND FAITHFUL." Revelation 21:4-5*

---

# AFTERWORD

When we welcomed a new family visiting our church one Sunday morning, I noticed that their oldest son was autistic. We already had one family with an autistic son and we loved them dearly. Their son and I had our very own special fist bump greeting. We let this new family know that they were welcome and that we would love and care for them all, including their special son. The last church they attended had informed them that they were no longer wanted there. Their son was too distracting to the service. I saw the fear of rejection and the uncertainty in their eyes. I quickly reassured them that this would be a refuge and haven for their family, all of their family. We love them dearly!

God loves all of His children. He created us all and knows us all better than we know ourselves. We are all beautiful to Him even though we are all unique. I would like to think He loves those who battle disabilities more than the rest of us and gives those who love them even greater strength and endurance.

Our capacity to love should be all encompassing. Denise has given us an insight into what it really means to love unconditionally, even when it feels like there is no hope. Thank you, Denise, for being brave enough to bare your soul for us to be able to catch just a glimpse of what it is like to love a son with special needs. Thank you for sharing your life with us all.

*Connie Bernard*
*First Lady and Wife of David K. Bernard, General Superintendent of the United Pentecostal Church International*

# AUSTISM RESOURCES

**Autism Speaks**
*www.autismspeaks.org*
Phone: 888-288-4762
En Español: 888-772-9050
Email: familyservices@autismspeaks.org

Autism Speaks has grown into the world's leading autism science and advocacy organization, dedicated to funding research into the causes, prevention, treatments and a cure for autism; increasing awareness of autism spectrum disorders; and advocating for the needs of individuals with autism and their families.

Autism Response Team (ART) members are specially trained to connect families with information, resources and opportunities. They are available to answer calls and emails from 9am to 1pm local time.

**Autism Society of America**
*www.autism-society.org*
Phone: 301-657-0881
800-3AUTISM (800-328-8476)
4340 East-West Hwy, Suite 350
Bethesda, Maryland 20814

The Autism Society, the nation's leading grassroots autism organization, exists to improve the lives of all affected by autism. We do this by increasing public awareness about the day-to-day issues faced by people on the spectrum, advocating for appropriate services for individuals across the lifespan, and providing the latest information regarding treatment, education, research and advocacy.

**Bancroft**
*www.bancroft.org*
425 Kings Hwy E
Haddonfield, NJ
Phone: 856-524-7322 | 800-774-5516

Bancroft is a leading nonprofit provider of specialized services for individuals with autism, brain injuries, and other intellectual or developmental disabilities. Bancroft has been assisting individuals and families with disabilities since 1883. Their programs include: special education, residential and community living, neurobehavioral stabilization.

**Cumberland Hospital for Children**
*www.cumberlandhospital.com*
Phone: 800-368-3472
9407 Cumberland Road
New Kent, Virginia 23124

For more than 30 years, Cumberland Hospital has helped children and families throughout the United States. Their Neurobehavioral

---∽∽∽---

*Visit*
*www.WHENGODSAYSNOBOOK.com*
*Tell your story.*
*Book a speaking engagement with Denise Wynn.*
*Schedule a life coaching consultation.*

---∽∽∽---

www.ingramcontent.com/pod-product-compliance
Lightning Source LLC
Chambersburg PA
CBHW071225090426
42736CB00014B/2973